The Old Refusals

Also by Carmen Germain:

Living Room, Earth

These Things I Will Take with Me

The Old Refusals

CARMEN GERMAIN

MoonPath Press

Copyright © 2019 Carmen Germain

All rights reserved. No part of this publication may be reproduced, distributed, or transmitted in any form or by any means whatsoever without written permission from the publisher, except in the case of brief excerpts for critical reviews and articles. All inquiries should be addressed to MoonPath Press.

Poetry
ISBN 978-1-936657-44-5

Cover art painting
Fantasia in the Key of Yellow
Carmen Germain
acrylic on canvas

Author photo by Tom Germain

Book design by Tonya Namura using Minion Pro

MoonPath Press is dedicated to publishing the finest poets living in the U.S. Pacific Northwest.

MoonPath Press
PO Box 445
Tillamook, OR 97141

MoonPathPress@gmail.com

http://MoonPathPress.com

Acknowledgements

In appreciation to these journals and anthologies in which my poems appeared:

Cape Rock: "Fields under a Stormy Sky"

Cider Press Review: "Wild Mind," "Color Is to Do Everything," and "What he claims is"

Common Ground Review: "This asocial assembly"

Comstock Review: "Reading *Aeneid* by Lantern Light" and "Potluck"

Crosscurrents (WCCHA): "Husband Wooing" and "Grand Mal, Florence"

Dos Passos Review: "A child runs into the street"

Fifth Wednesday: "Pelt Brandy"

Forgotten Women (anthology, Grayson Books): "The Dinner Table: Portrait of Camille" and "Olga Confronts Modernism" (reprinted from *Harpur Palate*)

Harpur Palate: "Olga Confronts Modernism"

Kerf: "Out of the Garden of Earthly"

Natural Bridge: "Guantanamo Prisoner Art, Camp Delta"

Naugatuck River Review: "After a Painting by Hans Holbein the Younger"

Northwind Arts Center, Port Townsend, Washington. Exhibit of poetry and art: "Installation: Domestic Interior." Broadside.

Poet Lore: "Coming Home, 1945"

The Sow's Ear Poetry Review: "Untitled: Distemper on Paper" and "Break Out"

Verse Wisconsin: "Declaration, Black Earth Farm" and "Journal: Rome" (originally published as "Art History")

Writers Harvest: "Suddenly at sunset" and "*La Cucina Povera*"

In gratitude:

Tom Germain, often the first audience for these poems.

Sally Albiso, for her close attention to my work, inspiring me with her fine poems.

Holly J. Hughes, for her generous reader's eye.

Tonya Namura, for her technical work and design expertise.

Lana Hechtman Ayers, managing editor of MoonPath Press, for her dedication in making poetry matter.

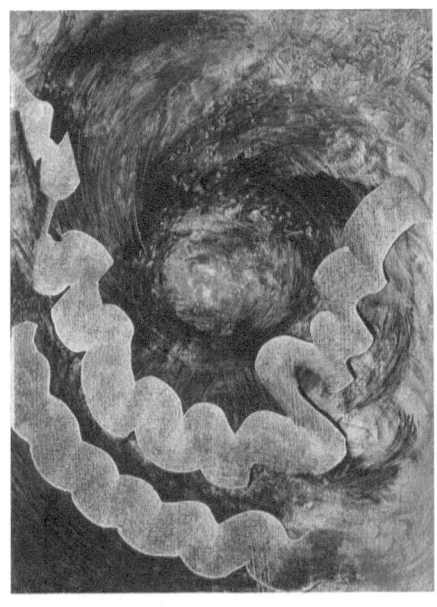

For Tom

And in memory of
Don and Frieda Kislinger

Sleep beloved in the dust of the Earth

Table of Contents

The Body's Leap
Out of the Garden of Earthly ~ 5
Like the first creation ~ 6
Pelt Brandy ~ 7
Declaration, Black Earth Farm ~ 8
Suddenly at sunset ~ 9
Wild Mind ~ 10
This asocial assembly ~ 11
Break Out ~ 12
Divine Hummingbird ~ 13
Mouse Remedies ~ 14

Inconstant Form
House in Winter ~ 17
Burning ~ 18
The doomed queen is outwardly stately ~ 19
Potluck ~ 20
On a Carved Gourd from Peru ~ 21
Highway of Tears, British Columbia ~ 22
Coming Home, 1945 ~ 24
Rut Season ~ 26
You calm the beast ~ 27
Husband Wooing ~ 28

What Abides
A child runs into the street ~ 31
La Cucina Povera ~ 32
Hoping for succor, ~ 34
Journal: Rome ~ 35
Funghi Mussolini (*A. Virosa*) ~ 37
A Coupling ~ 38
Reading *Aeneid* in Lantern Light ~ 39
Grand Mal, Florence ~ 40
Line from Book VI, *Aeneid* ~ 41

Color Is to Do Everything
After a Painting by Hans Holbein the Younger ~ 45
Las Viejas ~ 47
The Dinner Table: Portrait of Camille ~ 48
The Green Line: Portrait of Amélie ~ 50
Fields under a Stormy Sky ~ 51
About Her ~ 52
Olga Confronts Modernism ~ 53
What he claims is ~ 54
Untitled, Distemper on Paper ~ 55
Guantanamo Prisoner Art, Camp Delta ~ 56
Supplication, Chapala ~ 57
Color Is to Do Everything ~ 58
Installation, Domestic Interior ~ 59

Notes to the Poems ~ 61

About the Author ~ 63

The Old Refusals

The Body's Leap

Out of the Garden of Earthly

What is it watching held in its paws
the concrete cat on the concrete log?
Japonica shows ghost blossoms
later after we've lost this morning.
You know how honeysuckle sings
a spring day? That'll be gone, too,
down where the worm keeps vigil.
Far above us a passenger jet rumbles.
Remember how they taught us
to look up from this place?

So much *here*. Throw-away plantings
stumbling among
the migrations—bunchberry,
Solomon's seal, wild ginger
and juniper. Blue moon hosta
crowding shooting stars,
lemon bulb scenting
sweet woodruff.

I do what you tell me, bend my ear
near the bin with apple cores
and carrot tops, coffee grounds
and banana peels. Garbage sludge
a rich compost. And what you say
is true: red worms tangle sound
like nothing I've ever heard, suckling
honey from spring to mulch the beds.
I could reach in and lift a clump
of what we're done with, pulp
and seed and leaf, and from the bodies
of what they taught us to fear, such gold.

Like the first creation

the Expedition of Discovery
rode the Missouri with hunters and war
parties with slaves, farmers and mountain tribes.
Horse folk who humored the tall men passing
out medals, strange boasts from the *New Father*
where the long river started the morning.
Only fish and birds travelling back and
forth among the three levels of the world.
And when the man Lewis flushed free what he'd
never seen before, he'd kill and name it
describe feathers layered differently
in the West. How most of all he loved tongues—
delicacy of bison pulled from fire
how a *butifull red fox* got away.

Pelt Brandy

The grizzly sow hears my noise and charges
her cubs down the trail to the rancher's oats.
No one to stop this meal, rich grain holding
the cold to come where she'll slow her great heart
in a south-dug den. In daylight I find
her tracks, ten-inch pads pressing into earth.
And when I pass through underbrush, my neck's
a silver fox slinking alder, my throat's
a beaver, my mouth a mink, breath a lynx.
The kingdom of the wild lured you, New France,
into the forests of this world where you
broke the light from the body's leap, traded
brandy for pelts from trapper Indians—
reassembled the dead and the living.

Declaration, Black Earth Farm

Fierce, barking like feral dogs,
they hooked trotters over the half-door

of their shed if we got too close
as if to say hog meant more than smut

of shit on a snout. More than pink
hairless belly, smoke of cooking meat.

As if to declare in the swill of making-do
we, the unspeakable, speak.

Suddenly at sunset

it slammed the window full bird speed
switching lanes through trees

companion veering off and vanishing.
How could mountain summer snow

sweep of green and breeze between
suddenly forever darken this world?

Song thrush streaked gray and rust—
Pavarotti among the pop singers.

Where's the air so easily
ringing the forest in silver?

All's diminished, a snapped flute tossed
in the bushes with the leaves and worms—

Earth orbits a mechanical thing
and magic's just another dying star.

Wild Mind

and signs and abominations
and what we were born for, dogs

bouncing the fields—cur, mutt, stray.
When we find a few friends, we crash

through trees, when we taste blood
we're bound to it

and the night paces
the way it is, a fine excess of sound

and the river sings, walking
with the bear, living a long time alone.

We howl in this wild good fortune
sharpen our part of speech—

who goes there, the dead and the
living? And out of nature, yellow silk

of yard light, spilling *house*—

This asocial assembly

is gouging land for a private waterfall,
dragging boulders from the river for accent.
Snouts to the ground like hounds scenting deer.

Hounds scenting deer, tongues on the trail.
Gods in the thrall of genesis
skinning topsoil, rousing the sleep of bees.

Rousing the sleep of bees, shredding summer
by back-up beeper, startling the work
of creation. The ground nest revolting in riot

the ground nest rioting in diesel fumes.
Streets crushed by tracks. Buckets scooping
the steeples, the white porches, the homes.

Break Out

Leaving the ranch, the farrier horns through rumps
immovable as preachers, jerks the tight
lock-board loose from its gate rails, is on guard
for the free-for-all, the stampede out-bound
to the river he hears when the wind shifts.
Moose, grizzly, black bear, wolf own the land.
Now the rancher's son rides to the road head
on his quad, roars in high gear to the clot
of horses, stands as he whips in the heart
of them, scattering what blocks the way out.
The man taps thanks as he drives through
but they can't hear in their commiseration,
horses and boy held at the wild edge, brief freedom
fled. The slow movement of mountain ranges.

Divine Hummingbird

Lost from our life, too, someday. In Mexico
killed with bird shot the size of poppy seeds
or squeezed between human hands
or captured in fine nets. *Las chuparosas*
in botanica markets in Mexico City and border
towns, good luck spells or love voodoo
for widows, mistresses, and philanderers.
Men loveless in the plaza or women
trolling for husbands. Even the cartel
prays to the patron saint of safe travels
at the shrine where dead hummingbirds dangle,
red thread through eyes and throats, Aztec charms
and Catholic prayers for defense against police.

Glowing fire, Audubon wrote, *stretching out
its gorgeous ruff as if to emulate the sun.*
The Mexica plucked a blue and green helmet
of shimmering feathers and set it on the Sun God
to battle the stars and moon, and the bodies
of warriors flew into hummingbirds to serve him.
How this Rufous hummer's a blur at my window,
messenger from a world that forgets quickly.
Divine hummingbird with your holy power,
witches cram your magic in a vial of honey.
Divine hummingbird, forgive us our trespasses.
Hecho in Mexico slashed on satin tubes
hawked in the stalls. Forgive us our sins.

Mouse Remedies

In the seventeenth century, Topsell's
Four-footed Beasts offers a recipe
for keeping teeth into old age:
burn mice heads and grind the powder
for tooth-soap. To ease agony
if teeth beyond preserving, pull a tooth
from a live mouse and hang it
next to the rotten one in your mouth.
If you are shedding to bald
mix "mice dirt bruised with vinegar"
and rub well the paste on your pate.

Our mice shred felt and foam ripped
from the backseat, build a mound reeking
of litter after litter. The clerk selling traps
advises sew bacon on the metal spike,
mice adept at stealing cheese. But we lure
with Parmesan and Romano hard and salty
that can't be stolen without springing.

We'll drop the dead in the forest,
underbellies milky, black-seed
eyes shining in the moment
of snap and shiver,
prehensile feet pale
among berries and licorice fern,
foxgloves and maple.
Three teeth in a row to a cheek.

Inconstant Form

House in Winter

I think of Dersu, Siberian trapper
almost blind. Amur tiger prowling
hungry, too, musk deer browsing
the coarse brush under cover
of fir branches. How he sheltered himself
weaving grass thrust against the zero night.

~

On the sill aloe curves toward valley sun,
mountains scraping light
from brief days.
Yesterday the house stuttering
for an instant, machinery
stumbling off then on again,
somewhere a tree plucking lines.

~

In his weed cave Dersu slept
his animal sleep held fast by the bite
of ice. Knowing how easy it would be
to lie open to the land
and let come what comes.

Burning

Maybe she'd said to him, "OK, turn around,"
whiteout on the logging spur. Or they fishtailed,
bumper plowing snow drifts, reserved room rosy
from bed lamps sixty miles behind the Siskiyou.

And why did we do it, grind the jeep trail
with summer tires and rear-wheel drive
until we lost traction on the shortcut to Yosemite?
Sugar pines oblivious, cut bank crusted with ice,
car obeying physics: nothing to stop a body
sliding a precipice, mountain never backing down.
How you asked me to get out and wait
and if it came to that, hike out
with our terrible foolishness.

    And that family, after a week
burning tires. Like the Donner Party
damned in the dream of California, days worn hard
shuffling in circles. The animal curl of each child,
mother-milk in the den of the cab. On the ninth day
he tramped creeks to find cabins, skirt wrapping his head.
He thought a desert, stripped in freeze-up.

How is it we learn too late what falls from grace
is soon devoured? The way the Greenland Norse,
abandoned at last by the Viking supply ships,
lost their ancient fish-eating memory and starved.
Seed pile of wooden nails in flames
and nothing to burn on the edge of the sea.

The doomed queen is outwardly stately

clustering her subjects by the shipwreck—
the off-duty singer, the glassblower,
the waiter who comes to clear the plates.

Full of elegant repetitions,
she has the grin of an adman,
but no one believes the crisis is over.

Even experts lack expertise
and anyone listening in the hold
knows the flash drive's concealed in the cake.

How at the click of a button,
can opener, batteries, and flashlight appear.
Tins of soup and bottled water,

tranquil trickling sounds,
mechanics emerging from the pirate ship
like coins spilling from a purse.

Underneath the sea bed, buildings and rusty spoons.
Evidence of so many busy street corners
so many meals on the fly.

Potluck

News of his death like barbed wire
in the noodle stew, all of us

ladling from the common bowl.
No one shared some saved-up joke

or criticized a book.
Crows gathered, calling each

to each the old refusals.
How slowly talk returned

to what confounds the living—
bees foraging near an M & M plant

made blue honey, hummingbirds
memorized every flower,

Chinese archeologists
discovered 2,000-year-old soup.

On a Carved Gourd from Peru

Baskets of wool, bone-white.
Llamas loaded and blowing, roped
for the trail's descent.
A woman spooling crimson dye
from the cochineal beetle,
companions bending over grain
and a man tempering a flute—
all trouble my longing.
What I love, I will lose.
Seeds scooped, cavity-scoured
gourd sloughing to papery dust.
Because I had no child,
strangers one day
packing up the house—
And this— why did she keep this?

And this— why did she keep this?
packing up the house
strangers one day—
because I had no child.
Gourd sloughing to papery dust
seeds scooped, cavity scoured.
What I love, I will lose.
All trouble my longing,
and a man tempering a flute—
companions bending over grain.
From the cochineal beetle
a woman spooling crimson dye.
For the trail's descent
llamas loaded and blowing, roped
baskets of wool, bone-white.

Highway of Tears, British Columbia
How old is she? Oh? Just turned 18?
Give her a week. She's on a drunk.
—RCMP to mother of missing girl

No busses in the North and trusting in God,
girls hitchhike the Trans-Canada Yellowhead
past billboards of the dead and disappeared.

Girls thumbing
in the direction they think they're going,
travelling the wine of freedom—thinking nothing

happens to those who want nothing to happen.
How I felt at eighteen, the world eighteen forever.
Frog, bear, eagle on totems in the villages.

Slow work of moss, winter.
How cedar grays and splinters.
On the radio, the latest National Inquiry into Missing
Indigenous Women and Girls.

Shelly-Ann, 16.
Cicilla Anne, 15,
her cousin Delphine, 16, in the season of windflower.

Monica, 14.
Colleen, 16.
Monica, 12, in the season of shooting star.

We've been searching for eight years.

Loren, 15.
Nicole, 25.
Ramona, 16, in the season of forget-me-not.

We search the bush.
We search the mountains and valleys.

Tamara, 22.
Roxanne, 15.
Maureen, 33, in the season of death camas.

Pale-lilac, deep-purple lily
among the Indian hyacinth.
Life depending on what feeds, what kills.

Sun-bleached, gold-striped gown.
Red hoody, blue tank top on the billboards—
daughter lying on a bed, laughing.

We search the swamps
and marshes and rivers.

Gale, 19.
Pamela, 19.
Alberta, 24, in rain.

Leah, 15.
Kathryn-Mary, 11.
Gloria, 26, in ice fog.

Madison, 20.
Aielah, 14.
Micheline, 18, in earth freeze.

Coming Home, 1945

You sit on the stool with the sheet
on your shoulders remembering
your mother said curls on a man
were wasted, how women would die
for such hair. I snip and layer,
your mother long dead.

In the photograph with your father
before the war, her hair in waves.
She's small and thin and fashionable
on what she makes at the Jewish bakery,
daughter of Italian immigrants. Your father
a handsome heartbreak in a street-wise way,

parting the sidewalk where he walks.
Son of a bootlegger reduced to pennies,
quick and strong and ready,
fists famous in the South End.
In those days no one heard or saw
in the rowhouses planted cheek to jowl

when a woman with a bruise on her face
wept on the steps. It was nobody's business,
nobody's call, even if neighbor or sister or daughter
was slapped down last night in her own kitchen.
How could it happen that love wouldn't matter?
In the South Pacific he carried photos

of you and your mother,
waiting for peace against the odds.
Even now you see him bounding

the street from the taxi, snow in his hair,
your mother at the curtain, everyone
watching the father gone too long.

If that moment could have stayed—
how they looked at each other,
your mother with her lush waves,
your father, lean from time away—
you might have loved him,
might have mourned him, too.

Rut Season

On a neighbor's land, a man with a gun
where I walk to the river, woods busy
with hunters roaming for places to shoot.
In September, I startled the elk herd, three bulls,
harem of thirty. The cow with the red
radio collar loping off, the rest
hurtling steep down the bluff, the smallest bull
trampling and thrashing weeds, the biggest bull
trumpeting rack and muscle like the boy
in the pickup in town who screeched rubber
as shrill as Little Richard's squeal, teenage
girls shimmering on the sidewalk. How he gunned
the engine, swerved burning on all fours. Lust
undomesticated roaring twice its size.

You calm the beast

of adding and subtracting, reminding
me we'll suffer someday, face real sorrow
and in the world's great debits and credits
my failure to balance this checkbook pales.
But true mistakes multiply in shabby
coupling of mind and brain. How you never
found me out, your head deep under the hood—
fan blade still, some car swerving in moth light
not seeing us. It was like a lion
pounced my neck—and I forgot about you.
Leaped for the pedal, fight-or-flight, my sharp
hooves. Forgot the key had to be turned for
the surge. Jabbed in, almost caught the engine.
How gas-starved or flooded, it coughed, denied.

Husband Wooing

A warm summer night
when I wore this silky thing
sunk in the steamer trunk
twenty-five years ago, sure.

How August yields to August.
Tonight, you're downstairs
on the World Wide Web, courting
a turntable, a collector's deal

you don't want to lose,
downloading the what and how
and why. Looking in the mirror
I long for that other woman

how she could make you come
to her bed, the stars whirling,
the stylus stuck thumping
at the edge of a song.

What Abides

A child runs into the street

where I pounce
the brake, pound
the horn's shrill shout
ton of metal
veering off target
at the precise moment
she jumps back on the curb.

When quiet returns, living
rooms along the street still
flicker blue,
families gathered
as though nothing
could ever fall away.

It's true what they say—
travel changes you.

The guidebook to Rome's
splayed on the floor near
my right foot, passport
in its plastic case lost
under the seat.

It's the day before
my flight
from this mill town
on the Pacific coast
of North America

and I'm forced to face
the before and after
snake-
strike thought,
There goes Italy.

La Cucina Povera

Waxy as giant pears, provolone hangs sharp
making the mouth purse a vowel it can't finish,
string net tightening cheese in grooves
working in as weight slowly deepens.

Parmigiana for stuffed peppers and pesto, purple
nightshade pleasure, ricotta's creamy sweetness.
Dry Italian salami, mold peeling from paper skin
and when it's fresh, spices, wine and garlic
wrapped in a clean, bleached gut.

When you left the rowhouses for the city,
first paycheck weeks away, proud
and young and broke, you nursed a loaf
of Wonder Bread until you wore it out,
carton of milk freezing on the sill, winter

your first refrigerator. How every morning
you dreamed a shop where peaches tumbled
the tables, fragrant with sugar, lush
southern sun still swirling gold, and all
you had was hunger's currency.

Tissue-thin, prosciutto crudo cuts. Shriveled
black olives packed in rock salt, black Kalamata
from Greece, Sicilian cracked and dressed,
fennel seeds, garlic, olive oil. Oregano, tart.

    Tomatoes
only themselves, tired of names.
"Describe red," asked the blind man.
    Sun in your body, cells ablaze.

And *pane* smooth and round, twisted or split,
dipped in extra-virgin dark green first cold-press
        olive oil, taste closest to the fruit
and durum wheat semolina pasta unfurling
spirals and curls, angel hair and little hats.

Tonight, you bake manicotti Calabrese style
design antipasto on a clay plate
spoon sun-dried tomatoes on a bed of anchovies
olive oil glistening on roast peppers

La Cucina Povera—
the peasant kitchen

and lifting bread from stone
you call me to the table
of what perishes on this Earth
and what abides.

Hoping for succor,

the old priest shuffles like a man under water,
clutches bags of dogfish for feral cats
draping the American Academy in Rome.
Multitudes spring for the feast, gulls swooping

down in faith soon shooed. He stoops
to stroke an orange head, tawny pelt striped
like a Bengal tiger. Darting to umbrella pines
felinus hisses: never to be trusted—

kind voice, hands bearing such blunt confession—
blessings bestowed on those who give
to receive. It is said Francesco preached
and the wolf came to him. Song birds, gray crows,

and hawks. Silk and gold shimmering abandoned
in the house of his father. But what if *you* had a son
who sees a corolla glowing in the dawn
over slum dwellers, and he's called to joy,

says "nature's the mirror of God." Strips off
his wallet in full view of the neighbors. Hallucinates,
claims moon as sister, sun as brother.
Lives in a tent in the foothills, grows cabbages.

Tramps valleys singing to whoever will listen.
At night in his blankets punctures hands and feet
with a pocketknife. And say a thousand years pass
and say predators still prowl the flurry of wings.

Journal: Rome

Too young, they charged,
to have a grown son. But Michelangelo
defended his work—
"All virgins in their innocence
retain the purity of youth." How else

to quiet the critics? He knew
you were no simple woman.
How marble trapped you,
son collapsed in your lap
like a winter-sprouting lily.
Your beauty a star spill
broken open—
like the trillions of nights
    we'll never live to see.

~

The pantheon celebrated Jupiter
and at Pentecost the fire department
drops rose petals like tongues of fire
through the oculus. Golden arches
boast "One Million Served"
under the public service announcement
carved in marble by order of a caesar:
The people of Rome abhor
Vulgar commercial displays
That corrupt the beauty of art.

~

Galileo loved to talk, and Pope Urban.
Intellectual equals up all night
parsing Copernicus or the Greeks.

Imagine dinner with Galileo
as he laid the physics out.

Knowing the right fork
to use in argument,
which was wine,
which was water.

Then the descent back into darkness,
politics, and religion.

The universe he knew
before we came to see.

Funghi Mussolini (*A. Virosa*)

Per la storia! For history,
the vendor's quick to say. But why
the puffball-skull stamped
on faux gold watches? Imagine meeting
his jaw every time you checked
the hour. And that poster, would you

tack it on your wall, those Black Shirts
in goose step, hero fowl
squawking, saving the village from night
raiders? How he charmed Romans
from his balcony, saluting the future
of the broken, burning wall.

So graffiti on the gate of San Pancrazio—
Duce è Noi—
the ones who took root
in the gathering ground

the destroying angels
among the chanterelle.

A Coupling

Another quarrel. We're late for the train
to Ostia Antica—miss seeing
Keats's grave—touched off by fatigue, angry
in icy wind, wander the Egyptian
marble hidden in roughed-out quarry cuts
black and white mosaics of fish and wine.
"A Tragedy would lift me from this mess,"
the poet wrote, meaning money trouble
(life trouble came soon enough). You stumble
in rubble, sprain your wrist. Our apartment's
a din, sleep damned by sirens and Vespas,
your hand a bloated pomegranate. Love
carries the lover—the old blues tune—weight
of a river, bird with a broken wing.

Reading *Aeneid* in Lantern Light

When he began to look away after love,
she knew something was working in him
and remembered the cave's swirl,
the world tasting like a ripe, sweet berry.

She began brushing her hair in sunlight,
wanting its gleam of gold.
Began riding her mare hard,
hoping he'd desire how she rose

and fell against the beautiful roan.
When he rubbed his wrist and looked away,
she learned how blurred she was, how
breath was lost between coming

and going, between water and wave.
Later when Juno takes pity on her—
Dido dying unseen from his ship—
with a snip of the god-scissors

"All life went out upon the wind."

~

Snow overnight again, the Babine Range
woven by cloud bands. If I believed
in Jove, this is where I would seek him,
in these mountain caves. I'd tell him

it's torment enough
being human
but better than playing a god's game.

Grand Mal, Florence

Enough to say
his suede jacket is butter-
soft, his jeans a clean bit of sky.
I look and don't, scuffling past
as he writhes on stone

in March rain, mud and street grease
blearing him like bruises. Police
in the piazza work expertly,
let the storm blow
in the seizing so the rest of life

parts and flows around him.
But with this spellbound
companion, he's a ground
for the flashover that fells him
at the slightest provocation.

I think of being alone
these days hiking hills
above the town, the glint
of tusk in the old groves.
Wild boar grunting and gutting

trees in the bottoms of ravines.
Cambium scarred to the bone
and grass trampled,
the spring seep roiled
or about to be.

Line from Book VI, *Aeneid*
thinking of Sandy Hook

In the Palazzo Nuovo
2nd century BCE funerary hall—

Our sweet son
Aged six years, four months,
Three and a half hours,
Who had the intellect
Of an aged man, is crying
Now on his way to Hades

"Then on their ears a sound of wailing rose"—

Color Is to Do Everything

After a Painting by Hans Holbein the Younger

This is nothing new, how some are obsessed
by skulls blooming under every face
or grieve a flaming sunrise
decaying to night. Seeds
sprouting to compost, newborns
shrinking to crones. Birdsong
in spring the end of music
among the shedding maples. Nothing new

how the performance artist steps into bones
through hologram, strips his body
to essentials, fights the desire
to sleep in a coffin. Or the gallery
where I walk through mist—
water sterilized after washing corpses.
How I'm asked to confront mortality
as though it'd never entered my mind.

Nothing like the 16th century
where skeletons in woodcuts
drag bodies away by cowl or beard.
A mariner jostled in seas
where Death rows up in his bone cage.
A merchant tallying a shipment
where Death grabs a cape
and the merchant turns, arms raised.
Death scooping his worth in a basket
the seller flinging up empty hands.

In Holbein's double portrait
two men gaze at me. Bishop in collar,
ambassador in black velvet robe
lined with white fur, flute in hand.

On the mantel near where they pose, lute
with a broken string, globe, sundial,
crucifix. But what disturbs, as though
the painting plots five centuries ahead
where Dali's timepiece drapes a desert tree
and a pocket watch melts—
the gray and yellow distortion
growing from the bottom of the canvas.
An unknown grotesque, as if the artist slipped.

And the picture's meant to be hung
over a doorway where someone walking
would look up and pause, and there it is,
Holbein's optical trick revealing a skull—
like the bathroom mirror where I stare
half-asleep in the morning, body aging,
taking all that I'm given.

Las Viejas
That was when I understood
painting could be a language;
I thought I could become a painter.

Until then he believed
he'd never be able to paint
because he couldn't be like the others,
like Bouguereau—famous artist
of smiles and kisses, *putti*
and white doves and pink rose petals—
who told him he'd never learn to draw.

But startling, this trinity of Goya's
Matisse saw in the Galerie Véronèse—
two old women seated. Behind them
a hovering gray-haired spirit with wings
gripping a broom. The maid holding a mirror
to her mistress's fussy work
with hair and powder and ornament.

And this maid, eyes sunk in a soup-bone skull,
snout nose, broken teeth,
four rows of beads on her wrist,
peers aslant where the other gazes
at a withered, toothless jaw,
diamonds glittering in a dyed chignon,
arrow pinning the thinning yellow hair.

How the translucent gown of her mistress catches light,
lace and ribbons draping the crepe of body
and bones. *Que Tal?* on the back of the mirror—
How goes it? Time waiting
to sweep what's through.

The Dinner Table: Portrait of Camille

What would she do, another winter with no heat?
How Matisse never slept, worrying
about his paintings, other artists
starting to sell,
knowing what worked, and what didn't.
She must have begged him to think of his child.
How it would feel, pockets heavy with francs,
meat whenever they wanted.

Maybe she set it up, the still-life. Burnished
borrowed cutlery, porcelain, and glass.
Laid the tablecloth, bought fruit out of season
with whatever money they had. Hothouse lilies.
That winter he worked in coat and gloves
she posed as serving girl, and he meant it to be
real—colors subdued, knives painted
so sharp she might slice her fingers.
The way a feast for guests should look,
drapery gracefully muted, shadows curving fruit.

Meant it, this comfort—a complement
to de Heem's *La Dessert*, the opulence of a world
where there's always enough to eat.

But then peaches flamed crimson,
blushed orange, lemons deep
in pigment, wine carafes blooming
burgundy and cobalt, white highlighting white,
cloth brushed by saffron and ivory
with a band of red. And the serving girl
bending to fuss with the flowers?
Her face luminous in blue-violet.

Splendid color, anything he felt it to be,
not what it was. All the painting
dancing in front of his eyes, all he saw.

But I think of her, returning the bone-
handled knives, the plates and bowls,
butcher and baker holding out their hands
and the pears too ripe, bruised at the core.

The Green Line: Portrait of Amélie

When even making love wouldn't work
and he couldn't sleep, incendiary colors
exploding on canvas, she'd read to him
until early in the morning, maybe Dante
and Vergil among the Shades.

Maybe together they'd imagine Hell
for madmen who called *him* a lunatic,
a room carved in ice, walls glowing,
flame and freeze burning the same—
a place in Hades for detractors
who claimed people caught smallpox
standing too close to dotted brushwork.

A critic said, "The artist makes you see her
in a strange and terrible aspect," Amélie
not gazing at us, posing for Matisse
all those hours. Remembering him roaring
when he couldn't get light to dance on a tree.
An emerald mark splitting her, soft and hard.

Fields under a Stormy Sky

The same year van Gogh shot himself
behind a dunghill in a barnyard,
Hermann Corrodi painted *View of Corsica*,
a picture that sold. No tough island pony
stamping and sweating under saddle blankets,
only he climbed the hill,
palette and easel tied with rope
slapping his ribs on the narrow trail,
goat cheese wrapped in newspaper
apricots spoiling in southern sun
flies and gnats upwelling from broom.

Only serenity at the precipice of a chasm.
Barbary fig and rockroses in gray-green
and burnt sienna, vapor rising from the cleft
of cliff, sea and beach. Stone lighthouse.
Mountains framing sky, coastal jag below.
But no peril in this landscape, so unlike
van Gogh's cobalt-purple sky—
strange thunder falling to the field
empty of women or men. And waiting
for harvest, yellow slashes the horizon.
Turquoise flows green. Stabs of red
spike among wheat.

About Her

> *Everything is going black*
> *before my eyes.*
>   —Chagall, after the death of his wife, 1944

Zeuxis painted grapes so faithfully a dove
drifted from a cote to eat them. Above
the vines, the scent of dates.
Unforeseen in the old way of making
trick of hand and eye, an awakening
revision of the world.

O'Keeffe's deserts so luminous with light—
mauve cacti, cream corona, malachite
and lapis lazuli.
Joie de vivre in swaths of singing hue.
Jimson weed and rock hibiscus through
eye sockets and ribcage.

Before the death of his Bella, Chagall
painted laughing blue roosters dancing, all
interchangeable life.
Red cow, green violin, brides sweetly kissed.
Peasants without sickness from the artist
of fish-birds and bird stars.

False indigo, sea poppy, foam flower—
how we invent the world's color like sour
wears yellow for lemon.
But say it depends. Say grieving can gray
the visible spectrum, sorrow portray
a living crucifixion.

Olga Confronts Modernism

"As for me, I have no fear of art," Picasso said.

But how was it when she first saw *The Bathers*
the concave yellow of his lover's hair

how every oval offered a vagina, every
cabana the Minotaur's lair?

Near salt water, the sun
spread its red scarf

on a giantess and her sisters, thighs
massive as pylons of a wharf

and from a mirror of many colors
a girl with a belly of moon gazed at a man.

You can paint with whatever you want—
hooks and nails. The hearts of women.

What he claims is

true: death cap rises
after rain in the forest,
pits trap and vipers coil.
So Mondrian decrees
no fellow feeling beyond
geometry, admonishes
"contours of nature
should be tightened."

What is the tree to Mondrian?
Why does he so despise
the natural world
deny the red plum growing
outside his window, deride
the willow groves
close eyes to all that's wild?

"A drop of sperm spilt
is a masterpiece lost"
his gorgeously demented theory.
His art a box built to withstand
tough handling, unlike
the flame-red, blood-red rose.

Clear nights the Earth's
a flute of wine,
a near grave waiting,
while his *Flowering Apple Tree*
churns like terrible fish
riled in jacklight.

Untitled, Distemper on Paper
*Like catching a key to something.
That is what I feel when I draw.*
—Anna Zemánková, 1908-1986

At first, in her old age, corollas burst
from another planet: spiky orange fronds,
muscular and throbbing, devouring each other
splitting flesh petals. Her grown children

wanted to keep her occupied, suggested
she start painting again. How long ago
she dreamed of the art academy. Now
seeds pricked paper, rubbery tubes arose,

ochre swirling to brown striations
bulbous at tips with clusters of holes,
lotus pods resembling poisonous animals
like the deathstalker scorpion.

Purple brick walls growing leaves
red as clotted blood. Study dentistry
her parents must have said. You can't eat
paintings. Matisse's father wanted him

a merchant, Cezanne's groomed him
for the law. But how could she bear it—
those years of filling teeth, cleaning, drilling—
staring into what grinds, tears, and gnaws?

Guantanamo Prisoner Art, Camp Delta
It is forbidden to draw people,
portray identifying information,
see the work of others, or sign the art.

Consider a landscape, Ludwig Dill's
Birkenwald, the birch grove, 1900,
full summer leaf-stream, pale blue
sky like shredded silk between the forest's
dark colors—shadowy purple, maroon,
cold gray. Creek curving off the canvas,
yellow striking the trunks, last light's
swerve toward dusk. No figures or still-life—
only trees sharing sun, breathing serene,
the world lush before a war and waiting

and this watercolor painted more than
a century later. A man yet to be
charged, drawing behind a bolted door
in an art class for the guilty-until-proven.
His hand, too, follows shoals and ripples
vanishing in woods, marks of his brush
where he thought "here"—twilight's wash
like scorched butter. His cedar lying
broken. Crown split, the cut slicing the life-
root. The sunset hanging over the world.

Supplication, Chapala

Sketched on dog-eared paper
Our Lady of Zapopan, feet on a crescent moon.
Red tunic, mantle of gold, wide arc sparking
diamonds that made Indians
kneel before Spanish friars in New Galicia—
her image fashioned by Fray Antonio
from smoothed cornstalk and glue.

In the museum gallery, *Gracias* for grace and gift—
lineman scrambling off a burning pole,
rider limping from a motorcycle crash.
Fruit vender, grateful to have a living,
melons and mangoes piled in the market.
The Virgin hovering over a woman
in the hospital, arm pierced by a needle,
IV dripping. Pointing at the bed, a skeleton
in a white coat, flashing the smile of all skulls.

In the rainy season, bowl of fog over mountains,
the Queen of Jalisco's released from sanctuary.
Green kneels in fields after the long drought.
Paraded through streets, she visits barrios,
and plague flees, enemies collapse,
storms and lightning fade, floods cease.

How the ancients understood human blood
nourished the gods.
Silver and gold armlets of priests,
pearls, turquoise, and jade glinting
from a thousand steps, egrets silent in reeds.
Coatlicue, Lady of the Serpent Skirt,
wearing a necklace of mangled hearts and hands.

Color Is to Do Everything

Five days of rain and now this clean morning
pulse of pure light—luminous on the sill
the peacock plume's iridescent blue-green.
"Whenever I gaze at it," said Darwin,
"makes me sick," its inexplicable art
grounded in the functional universe.
Silent chickadees stab gray weeds for seed.
By noon leaden clouds weigh the valley dull.
Battling gloom, I load my brush yellow,
wild hue burning like southern sun. Why we
stirred red ocher with bison fat, painted
Lascaux with reeds, and pebbles shaped like birds.
Shells evolving from the limestone oceans
to bones, to hands that abandoned the sea.

Installation, Domestic Interior
—after a line by André Breton

Like larkspur emerging
upside down—
flowers buried in earth
roots burned by sun—

I lose myself
gazing at these sagging
Persian rugs and suspended
tables and chairs,
step around chandeliers
and sprinkler systems,
stoop to touch roof beams,
stretch to reach
the hanging couch.

When at last the house
is silent of you
it will be like this,
uncertain where I am
the way a winter moth
flits the crack of light
in night's window,
surprised by the disguise
of darkness, the treason
of tangible things.

Notes to the Poems:

"Out of the Garden of Earthly" is for Laura. "Down where the worm keeps vigil" is a line from Thomas Wolfe.

"Wild Mind" and "The doomed queen is outwardly stately" use techniques of collage and cut-ups from random sources. As Tony Hoagland wrote, "Collage is ... antirational and semi-intentional,...takes coincidence and chance materials as part of its method and inspiration" (qtd. in Edward Hirsch, *A Poet's Glossary* 216).

"Reading *Aeneid* by Lantern Light": "All life went out upon the wind" is the last line of Book IV.

"The Dinner Table": Camille was a lover of Matisse in his early years and the mother of his daughter. Provincial middle-class families didn't recognize their Left Bank artist sons' mistresses but depended on these young working-class women: sons living in Paris would be taken care of until marriages were made with respectable women. The future for the unmarried, single mother could be grim.

"The Green Line": Amélie was Matisse's wife.

"Olga Confronts Modernism": Olga was Picasso's first wife. The reference "concave yellow" refers to one of Picasso's many mistresses, Marie-Thérèse Walter, who was seventeen when she first lived with the artist. Picasso often referred to himself as the Minotaur.

"Color Is to Do Everything": The title is quoted from a letter of Vincent van Gogh.

"*La Cucina Povera*" and "Installation: Domestic Interior" are for Tom. "The treason of tangible things" is a line from André Breton.

About the Author

Carmen Germain grew up near the Mississippi in rural Wisconsin. She lived and worked in Washington, D.C., Montana, and California before making her home in Washington State in the upper Elwha River valley, Olympic Peninsula. She taught at Peninsula College, Port Angeles, for over twenty years where she was a co-director of the Foothills Writers Series.

Holding degrees in literature from the University of California, Santa Cruz, and the University of British Columbia, she is the author of the chapbook *Living Room, Earth* (Pathwise Press) and the collection *These Things I Will Take with Me* (Cherry Grove). *Cider Press Review* nominated her work for Best of the Web in 2016; she has received a Washington Community Colleges Humanities Association award for poetry. The anthologies *In a Fine Frenzy: Poets Respond to Shakespeare* (University of Iowa Press) and *New Poets of the American West* (Many Voices Press) as well as the journals *Flyway, The Madison Review, Cold Mountain Review, Poet Lore,* and *Natural Bridge*, among others, have published her poems.

During her time as a visiting artist/scholar at the American Academy in Rome, she researched the work of post-war novelist Elsa Morante; some of the poems in *The Old Refusals* had their genesis in Italy. Germain's work is influenced by Italian/American culture, especially the Little Italy that was once alive in the South End of Albany, New York, as well as Upper Midwest farm culture and the wilderness of northern British Columbia. Ajijic, Jalisco, Mexico has a presence in her work. In addition to learning from poetry, she is also a visual artist.

www.ingramcontent.com/pod-product-compliance
Lightning Source LLC
Chambersburg PA
CBHW030130100526
44591CB00009B/595